GOAN ATOM

GOAN ATOM
1. DOLL

Caroline Bergvall

KRUPSKAYA • 2001

ACKNOWLEDGEMENTS

Early versions of this text have been published as "Les jets de la Poupee" (1998) in *The Oxford Anthology of Twentieth Century British and Irish Poetry*, ed. Keith Tuma (NY: Oxford University Press, 2001) and in book-form as *Goan Atom: 1. jets-poupee* (Cambridge: rem press, 1999). Many thanks to Keith Tuma and to Lucy Sheerman and Karlien van den Beukel for supporting this work, and to the Krupskaya editorial team for enabling this final version. Many thanks also to cris cheek. "Gas" was initially written for the sound-text collaboration *Ambient Fish* commissioned by Hull Time Based Arts and developed with Lewis Gibson for Root'99. Thank you beppa1952. Thank you John Tranter/*Jacket*, Suzanne Zelazo/*Queen Street Journal*, John Stammers/*Magma*, Loss Pequeno Glazier/*EPC*.

Flipbook - Gertrude Stein, *How to Write*: Dolls should be seen.
Backcover - Drew Milne: "A veritable dollmine: Caroline Bergvall, *Goan Atom, 1. jets-poupee*", Quid #4 & Jacket #12. Frank O'Hara: "Memorial Day 1950".

Cover Art, "Green Nip", from the electronic text piece *Ambient Fish* by Caroline Bergvall
Cover Design by Frank Mueller
Typesetting by Caroline Bergvall and Jocelyn Saidenberg

Distributed by Small Press Distribution, Berkeley
800-869-7553
orders@spdbooks.org

ISBN 1-928650-08-2

KRUPSKAYA
PO Box 420249
San Francisco, CA
94142-0249
www.krupskayabooks.com

Arrhe est à art ce que merdre est à merde

(Duchamp)

Anybod's body's a dollmine

•	T	S
S	S	O
G	G	F
C	A	A

S	S	•
G	T	S
O	A	A
C	F	G

gasp sag toga goat gag cot go cat fag fog tao sat as tag at ass fast

19 45 61

S

G

O

C

Enters the **EVERY HOST**
dragging a badl Eg
Finally !
So that the inspiration for such thoughts
becomes visible through the navel in order
To take advantage of the interior mechanism
run through the thoughts retained of little girls
as a panorama deep in the belly
revealed by multicoloured electric
illumination
it's roped in bottoms up I want to
B ba
b bo
b be
b leed
the load
o
Ff***
Mud and Dead
the mud offal the dead
stuffed goat much
Junk & Gusto
Whats looking at me
Form Form Form
one hardened core after another
bleeding harp
PushPushMarquis
or PunchOlichinelle
Skin-sacks
Minor monticulates
lined Up joind by hind thoughts

OFART
Eat Shit gladly

both sides Atlantic
Forte love
Forte loot
o found ConCubicles
Some Fav affemmée
an Ourite's Belle
y firms Con-Con
poupée de çuir poupée de çon
Cuillère des Spoons orifficielles
the opening circa of my
Flask and Blood
(something outstandish about this bene
fits from micro-friction)

Her e commaes
(Such Heir Hair Errs Airs)

Enter **DOLLY**
Entered enters
Enters entered
Enter entre
en train en trail
en trav Ail Aïe
La bour La bour La bour
wears god on a strap
shares mickey with all your friends

Sgot
a wides lit
down the lily
sgot avide slot
donne a lolly to a head
less cin
dy slots in

        to lic

Kher shackle
good dottersum
presses titbutt
on for the Puppe's
panoRama

nic
e round
ed olly

Woo pops
er
body partson
to the flo
ring the morning
it’s never matt
ers what goes back
on w
here Dolly
goodolly
in a
ny shape or form

Wit one fine toast
erin the belly
wit no head
wit nos
ticky hairs
round the folly
and nof ingers at the tips
(or more)

likes hang
in
from the trees with
herl egs up in the air
egs dowhile her l
non
the ground

indy

Li
kemy dolly's knees t
Hey full of joins
they're full of joi

N

N

S

S

S

N

s

E

s pleine didely

Suc ha

clever holly
polie penny

sits on the cha
irk daisy
stickin gout
and a big bal
looms in the cranny

Wit ak not for the
hair sometimes blond
sum tied black again
st st
the wallpaper
or across
thes heets

E

Sgot uP
elvis
(point to the Intero)
question mark

In a big way in
sclamation mark

Fact e’s got
2
and a central boule

Shorts white ocks
end black shoes
for girls when e goe
e goe Sout in the w**oo**ds
in the dark
in a large coating
Watch baby hind the trees
P
ouch
contract a bunny ride
on sweaty bice
ickles your
UCH hairy cr
up

Still
a dirty doldo's
one fatpig
fruitcake
in the bowl of my pill
ow naughty bumps
yternally croks
my rip
the stickout grappe
of your naval ma d'olliv ery bad
storms today
very bad

DOLLY
Tank-up !
This is the & of the world

s

T S

A

F

E

Enter **HEADSTURGEONS**
followed by
Enter **FISHMONGRELS**
colon speech marks
Trouble in the Hous
?
illy all tied up

Nothing random
says the **EVERY HOST**
about the herrings of this
fanny face
Once remove
able envelope
just stamp
or aply
anywhere
Twice culled more lovéd

All presently engage in a
(vigorous)
POINT-DE-DEUX

What of it
bodymass is heavily funded
Swirling aHeads
roll out of place
mount alterity
part on display
round up
to as perfect a square as Octopus
ever canned
be
roll on roll on
MOTion
begs out of

g
GA
g
ging
Dis
g
orging
b
loo*
p
uke
s
Uck
ack
ock
S
OG
ex
B Creme
ental
eaT
ing sp
Am
mon
Am
mon
sp
you
d out
the 1 called
and one called
wholly
quartered
Beloved
Beloved

chok
en the Egg
SP
in
your arm
to ram
my Hoop
of larm
b
(click)
L**oo**k
!
You Yo
Footy
facey
(click)
yoyo
and a leg loops
into the
BAC of the
my
thRoat
and Ro
und and Ro
und and the Rolling Eye up we gl gloue
in the bl**dy dans hole

UNICA-HOUSE

(Homage Louise Bourgeois)

“consequently
it was necessary to spend some time in the vaults of the head
because that is where the fever really
c
omes to fruition
”

CINDY UNTIED # 250

Bah Bah
By ba
Ba by
Baby a-hole is some
Fairground to limins as these
Easy not to know
which is when
& where is which
Before in after-breach
Baby baby
Catch your
Skin a collateral
Screwed into one sprawled
live-sized granpa
with a liver no
blood pud
no
rganic drill
do up e's mule

Never make dolls
full st
upscales
A CO CALLED MOO
Dolls should be seen full st
They should be gathered op op
They should be op With all my
H
H
eart

LIFTING a large coming
into this massive evide
dented continues

Outspell each one of my sweet fear abouts
crossing the
BIG TOE
D of Battle
sclamation mark

DOTTER
warf warf laffing
sucking on Lolly
swings a medoly

Mater Regina
was my First kiss
not my 2nd
Yet the shadows flourish

Mater Regina
was my First V
not my third
nor my 4th nor my 5th

Mouth in a mool
Mool in a bloom
Mater Regina
was my first Gash
not my last

(Sudnly arrosed exclaims)
NO
workable pussy
ever was su
posed to discharge at will
all over the factory
sclamation mark

AH YES
puts in the **EVERY HOST**
but sheeped
like a dolly
part out part ed
partout prenante
every little which way
right through the mid-
Come ‘n
gain a bit
Come a kiss
(is made of this)
: it’s a girl
Come a kiss
: and it’s not
In fact it was
inconvenient
colon italics
Come again a bit freddy
(Nov 18 1819)
to mate a door
in creset drawers
turn & turn the public lays

It must be humbly AD-
Mary by the lake
had a good
idea that is
“by some law
in my temperature”
quote MITTED invention does not consist
in cric-crac
crrr crr
ee
a ting out of void
but out of the ka
bone of insecting
rooms unquote

Meaning comma
if we be wet in church
my sweet inventory
hol da
headup inflate
my lily pousse my bridal suite
every mouth is ador
every little blood
draws
out another
casing

Blt **o** by Bolt
Every single P
art is a crown
to Anatom

u

Loose all the parts
will have a funded funk

Doll y had a gold gueule & a belle mine

Throws up in the air
Turns a pack of light
into a kit of bloodbone
A rouse ! these crops

Fan out
aslow assem
Press out theYe
loocked up in kyhole
of this pandOrama

& the Mouth sHits out th Eye
Ambient Eye Amphibic Eye surRound

A very slow dissem
qui saime d'issem
assem d'issembl

shits th Egg in th Eye
Eye under Skin
press out
fan out

& the Mouth shits th Eye
Pun sPinning
in my Poussy Yolk
and my Hoily Boule

jette jets P
youpee splattering abouts
the b**ody study of a sacred pear

DOLLY (in bits)
Let Theart bod y M !

& THEARS clickage & THe ighs come to

H

•

S

A

G

s

Abodys a corps
Abody sa corps is cur bed
lie in it

Says the **EVERY HOST**
For whom still sleeps encore in bod
in your bed Y vient in corps
Make fl
esh sometimes much agreed
encore encore !
in corps accord
mate loot with loot

Yet mostly corps à corps
loot mate with mate
A corps is a unit a detachment
a body's a corps disagreed
corps aggravé
tiréd in the flèsh

Also a detachable unit
aggrieved pried open
bloodied at corps
in bled in corps
then left for d**d

Unearthed
then stuffed for gain
If only bodied
and stuffed with fear
& the d**dman cRied as was laid to rest
who bled ry
pulling on this tired fleece

Time again
temps for the body of un corps

For the corps of a body body
For the body of a bod
Y bod Y bod

For a bod makes corps
not abode
Yet in body
Yet uncorps aboding

Uncorps d'encore
Un corps des corps
Decorpsed décorps
Decamps
echancre et d'encres au ventre
ride ride
for a being time another walkabout

A tabled **GROUP OF CORPOREALS**
Fitscrewed Facial sites
Big coily brains
throbbing ambient genitals
swooning in cans of fish
swap heads all sitting on long brooms couldn't agree more
colon speechmarks
"Th brood would be swept clean out"
"Sweeping the brood clean out"

Blood has been wept off the lot
Pear-shaped machineries
that cruise one another's defaced milkmachines
Slip on a slap on a Chatte Cat upfront
to sleep with Broad Loot
Outbroads La-Bonkings
Hefty lab onktonk ad hoc rigged up
shag the rut all butts too shine
fruit heavy A collection of holes
bafr to ckont indifferently hanging at one an other's throat
Meatpunk Gurgoyle Dirdymussel Brandmass Membrine Upmushdbudglov
Horrible languages outcries of woe
accents of anger Voices deep and horses with hands
smut together that swelled the sound of
the tumult through that air with solid darkness

I'm still bringing them through gently
says the **EXPRESS COACH**
I expect them to train as hard as I did
but they can't because their bodies aren't
Ready For It yet

Compact jars of body conc
crack op

-Entrate **SLOB**
w/Corporeal entourage
Teeth hanging by the crowns
Boof boof speaks
des trous des airs des enfilades
Half-wriggle half-hook
half-spittle
at the limits of perusal
Des compressions
Des arrois
Rejects of form
Oratorical bypass colon
Mankind, that's me
sclamation mark

S

Peak at twenty-odd
Lean on facts in favour in cited
Hold on to pRoven limbs when hitting on
drifting object mater

RELAX
permutate activating the lever vibrates right into the skull
provides very large w
inks anks

Eat change
Peer litter
Say Mma
Say Ppa
Spend the rest of this waking life catching up as in
Poking faeces with a stick

WHY does filiation impress us so quote unquote
I've been collecting hooks for relics
The supposition is that the oldest [sens du mot] is the nearest to
truth or recalls what has been lost

All in all move about en mass
Best not go it on one's own
One bad swipe leaves much to be disgussed

Some double-headed
in charge of sofening landscapes
t ween th dead th live th10-digitalisd
Conversit in landing pouches

“What drives a half-leg ?
“There’s hairs on that calf !
“Needled through one by one must
“**Likelihooded !**
“I want some !
“?
[Verisimilitude]

And each one by one
Gober that one up

Wipes a good few
c
L lean out of the Ff
rame Jump !
(I was pushed)
fall out of the flot
into a collectively blank

Get-Off

Bang Bang the Bell
Y goes pop incessantly

Day in day out
the sound of bon hitting hom
Limns itching each rep: eatedly: resented
Dup onder Licate at will
Air compacted for ays and Eeks
boom Blows up the bloody mooning
from the mid out

THE ARTIST
as archivist as archaeologist as bricolist as cataloguist
as collatist as collectist as compilist as ethnographist
gathers up the debris particles
as residues as indices
hung from wire
lit from centre

A SCALE OF TEATS
(14 juicy and penetrating in all things)
Alloy
Alloy
the spc is full of slosh and form

[praise knees d]

Enter Clac-Clac Clac-Clac
CHORUS A SCHOOL OF TEETH
head for a croupe
and a croupe for a neck
speechmarks
Nothing can compare
to te icdil of body past
humanolo clac
crowded physiques wat mumbl "vaseline"
and mount one a noter's rising
melanclac cholia

MERCHANTS
Fuck skin
The ternal is urgical
Is the ternal urgical
Animated turn
tables patent Ason
from a boxo orgns

A SCHOOL OF TEETH
Icdils of summer clac
Fish are flying
and te living is easing
Lazy pick-nooks in
te fat green of feels
clac postules

MERCHANTS
We're not acturally
against skin
worn long in season

AND ALL PRESENTED ream on one elbow

Praise knees d
Praise knees d

One elbow
to elbow
b-
Ack-to

(ife)

th absent Loeuf — that merry L-ip

breaks off the cuff
intones an opera
tive mouthful
flayed lengthwise

Ambient fish fuckflowers bloom in your mouth
Ambient fish fuckflowers bloom in your mouth
Ambient fish fuckflowers bloom in your mouth
Ambient fish fuck flowers bloom in your mouth
Ambient fish fuck flowers loom in your mouth
Alien fish fuck fodder loose in your ouch
Alien fish fuck fodder loose in your ouch
Alien fuck fish fad goose in your bouch
Alien phock fish fat geese in your bouche
Alien phoque fresh fat ease in your touche
Alien seal fresh pad easing your touch
To fish your face in the door
a door a door
fuckflowers bloom in your mouth

Ambient fish fuckflowers bloom in your mouth
Ambient fish fuckflowers bloom in your mouth
Ambient fish fuckflowers bloom in your mouth
o
Ambient fish fuck flowers bloom in your mouth
Ambient fish fuck flowers loom in your mouth
Alien fish fuck fodder loose in your ouch
Alien fish fuck fodder loose in your ouch
Alien fuck fish fad goose in your bouch
Alien phock fish fat geese in your bouche
Alien phoque fresh fat ease in your touche
Alien seal fresh pad easing your touch
To face your fish in the door
ador ador
fuckflowers bloom in your mouth

will choke your troubles away
will choke your troubles away
will choke your troubles away
will shock your double away
will soak your dwelling away
suck rubble along the way
suck rubble a long way
suck your oubli away
watch a getting a way
watch a ramble away
take the gamble away

will choke your troubles away

will choke your troubles away
will choke your troubles away
will choke your troubles away
will shock your double away
will soak your dwelling away
suck rubble along the way
suck rubble a long way
suck your oubli away
watch a getting a way
watch a ramble away
take the gamble away

choke your troubles away

AND ALL PRESENTLY

have never felt so close to wanting a
Heart to boot
is fast becoming
The latest continent around

a

DOLLY

Kss my fr
og
ock
Rub the genie tales
Some dream off kin
for kind
want a better make
another and-and
and and and and
“finely structured mesh”
“suitable scaffolds”
seed a kleenex today
to marrow the world
much like
“growing an arm and hand”
mol assumule eculargesse
bandaged on
not born slurpy
quote Someday Independent
22 Febr 1998
“The hurdle is nerve tissue”

Much in it who saw som ingle withe Postfaced
Dotted in small groupings
mooch about mocks a Vie
Garbs root garbs for routes

workit baby

and the spac eB ween's solids
& the spac in solDis peed s Peech